JACQUES PRÉVERT

SELECTED POEMS

Translated by
Sarah Lawson

Hearing Eye

2002

Published by **Hearing Eye**
99 Torriano Avenue, London NW5 2RX

English language translation © Sarah Lawson 2002
Introduction © Sarah Lawson 2002

ISBN 1 870841 96 4

These poems appear in the following volumes, all
published and copyright by Editions Gallimard: *Paroles,
Spectacle, Le pluie et le beau temps, Histoires et d'autres
histoires,* and *La cinquième saison.*

Front cover photo of Jacques Prévert by Jacques Robert,
© Gallimard. Back cover photo by Sarah Lawson.

This publication has been made possible with the
financial assistance of London Arts.

Typeset by Daniel James at mondo designo

Printed by Catford Print Centre, P.O. Box 563, London
SE6 4PY.

CONTENTS

From *D'autres histoires*

From *La cinquième saison*

INTRODUCTION

When Jacques Prévert's first book of poems, *Paroles*, was published in 1946 it was an instant hit. Until then he had been known in the cinema world as a screenwriter and in Paris cabaret circles as a songwriter, but now his fame spread throughout France as an anarchic, post-surrealist poet. At a time when serious poetry had to be as obscure and exclusive as possible, Prévert's work struck a chord with all his readers and made no claims to be 'literary' or to require extensive background knowledge. It was committed, imaginative, and entertaining.

Jacques Prévert was born in Neuilly-sur-Seine at the western edge of Paris in 1900, the son of a ne'er-do-well journalist, André Prévert, and his wife Suzanne. Jacques was the second of three sons. His elder brother Jean died of typhoid in 1915. Jacques remained very close to his younger brother, Pierre, all his life and in adulthood they often worked together on films.

Jacques' paternal grandfather, Auguste Prévert, was a stern and forbidding presence in the family and was probably the source of much of Jacques' later hostility to authority figures of all kinds. Jacques' father had already reacted against his father's strict ways. Although Auguste was a staunch Catholic, André was so lax about his sons' religious upbringing that Jacques was about to be confirmed at school when it was discovered that he had never been baptized. Auguste Prévert was also the head of the Paris department of poor relief and once helped out his impoverished son by appointing him to a post interviewing the poor to establish how deserving they were of public welfare. Young Jacques went along on these house calls, and it is tempting to find the origin of some of his later subject matter here.

Jacques disliked school (as is evident from several of his poems), and his father helped him play truant by telling his teachers that Jacques was needed at home to look after his poor invalid mother. Madame Prévert was perfectly healthy, but was as easy-going as her husband about matters of discipline. Prévert's criticism of the authoritarian school regime of his day has been noted by the descendants of those hated authority figures, and now there are numerous schools in France named after Jacques Prévert!

Prévert left school as soon as he could, but was always an avid reader and educated himself in the things that interested him. He worked briefly in a Paris department store and had a stint in the army (in Constantinople in 1920-22) before falling in with a group of young radicals who had decided that work was to be avoided at all costs. Fortunately for them, one of their number was the son of a rich hotel-owning family who spent his days in striped trousers on the Right Bank and his evenings with the budding surrealists in their squat on the Left Bank. Every evening Marcel Duhamel brought with him platters of food from the hotel kitchens. The young rebels feasted every night on the same fare as the customers of the upmarket Hotel Wagram in the rue de Rivoli.

Jacques seems to have had a great talent for friendship and was the centre of this group of a dozen or so who began to call themselves 'the Lacoudem', which they said meant 'those who greet each other by rubbing elbows'. The Lacoudem were madcap bohemians who gave each other outlandish nicknames and were fond of practical jokes. They would often stage little impromptu 'happenings' in the cafés they frequented or in the street with unsuspecting strangers. Within the group lovers and spouses were acquired or exchanged with general good-will all around. The same group of friends evolved into the 'Groupe Octobre', named after the month of the Russian Revolution. Prévert had begun to write the words for semi-dramatic performances for it; there were costumes and scenery and some acting-out, but the group also chanted the words as a chorus. The subjects of these performances were usually anti-military, anti-authoritarian, and anti-capitalist. Although Jacques Prévert was always too wary of regimentation to join anything, including the Communist Party, most of the other members of the Groupe Octobre were either members or in strong sympathy with the regime in the Soviet Union and with the Front Populaire in France. The Groupe Octobre performed in Moscow in 1932 at an international festival of workers' theatre and won first prize for a piece called 'The Battle of Fontenoy'.

On the outbreak of the Second World War in 1939 Prévert avoided the immediate call-up by quickly arranging to have his appendix removed. Later he was delighted to learn that he had a thyroid abnormality that rendered him unfit for military service. He left Paris when the Germans were about to take it. Many Parisians fled by the mainline train stations and the major roads out of the city. Prévert and a few of his friends, Parisians born and bred, fled by Métro, taking a train to the end of the line and then continuing by various means until they reached Jurançon, far to the southwest, where other friends owned a large estate.

Prévert and his group soon moved to Marseilles, to which much of the Parisian intelligentsia had repaired, and then to St. Paul de Vence. Although Prévert knew and supported many members of the Resistance and protected his Jewish friends and colleagues, he was never an active member of a network. He seems to have kept a low profile while helping his friends avoid being arrested or deported, like Joseph Kosma, the Hungarian Jew who set many of his poems to music. He hid them, helped them get the right identity papers, or found work for them. Active Resistance work would have gone against his pacifist and anti-militarist convictions. (He was later criticised for not taking a more active part in the French Resistance, but his critics misunderstood his deeply ingrained pacifism.) In any case, his detestation of both Nazism and Marshall Pétain's Vichy government were evident in his writing. Prévert and his Parisian film-making friends continued to make films in the south of France, the best known being 'Les Enfants du Paradis' in 1943. During the Occupation some of his poems circulated secretly. Their audacious snook-cocking gave many French people courage during those trying times. After the War when his editor was collecting copies of Prévert's poems, many copies came to light because French civilians had been gathering in clandestine groups to read and secretly enjoy these impudent anti-authoritarian poems. Other poems had been published in small magazines or given to friends for their own amusement or written to be sung or chanted and never previously published. Before *Paroles* could come out, it had taken the combined efforts of many friends, acquaintances, readers, fans, and colleagues from Groupe Octobre days to locate the songs and poems of the previous 15 years.

Post-war France loved *Paroles*. The first edition of 5000 sold out in a week. Other volumes followed in the 1950s and 1960s, containing more gleanings from the past and some new work. However, in October 1948 Prévert suffered an accident that was like some strange event in one of his poems. He fell out of a first-floor window overlooking the Champs-Elysées and received such a serious head injury that he was in a coma for 10 days. As a result he was prevented from working for two years and went back to the south of France to recuperate.

Prévert never called himself a poet or his writings poetry. When he was reminded that the Larousse dictionary called him a poet, he just shrugged. In the mid-1950s he ceased film-making except for the occasional short. In the later years of his life he became increasingly interested in collages, collecting images and then assembling them in surrealistic ways, just as his words, too, were often surrealistic collages. His books of what he called writings but everybody else called poetry continued to sell well, and now the sales figures have topped 3 million.

His last years were blighted by lung cancer, which he contracted after a lifetime of smoking three packs of cigarettes a day. Jacques Prévert died in 1977, leaving Janine, his third wife, and their daughter, Michelle.

Prévert's work is characterised by great playfulness and inventiveness, but an underlying seriousness. True to his surrealist past, some poems take a dark, menacing turn. Others feature bewildering, dream-like transitions. His texts are full of puns; some are large-scale puns, like 'The Musicians', which is based on the dual meaning of *l'orgue de barbarie* (a 'Barbary organ' or hurdy-gurdy or, alternatively, a 'barbaric organ'), or visual puns as in 'The Supper' where a dinner plate becomes a halo, or even little jokes like 'The Betrayed Lovers', which is completely untranslatable, but I have tried anyway. There are not many English translations of Prévert, perhaps because his puns and wordplay ensure that much of the effect of his poems will be lost in translation unless the translator can find some equivalent wordplay. Other poems are attached to their time and may be of more historical than literary interest.

This volume contains poems and short prose pieces from five of Prévert's published collections. I have tried to select pieces that demonstrate his typical concerns and styles. I have added a few notes at the end of the texts to clear up puzzling references or to give background information.

Sarah Lawson
London, 2002

11

THE HORSE'S STORY

Good people, hear my lament
hear the story of my life
I speak to you as an orphan
who is telling you his little troubles
gee up...
One day a general
Or rather it was one night
a general actually had
two horses killed under him
those two horses were
gee up...
how bitter life is
it was my poor father
and then my poor mother who had hidden under the bed
under the bed of the general who
who was hiding behind the lines
in a small town in the south.
The general was talking
was talking to himself at night
was talking in general about his little problems
and that's how my father
and that's how my mother
gee up...
died one night of boredom.

For me family life was already finished
leaving the bedside stable
I fled at a full gallop
I fled toward the big city
where everything was bright and shining
in moto I arrive by Sabi in Paro
excuse me I was speaking Horse
one morning I hoof it to Paris
I ask to see the lion
the king of the animals
I get whacked with a shaft

on the side of my nose
because a war was going on
the war that was continuing
they stuck blinkers on me
so I was mobilised
and as there was this war
this war that was going on
life became dear
the food got scarce
and the scarcer it got
the more the people looked at me
with a funny look
and teeth that chattered
they called me *beefsteak*
I thought it was something in English
gee up...
all those who were alive
and stroked me
waited for me to die
so that they could eat me.
One night in the stable
one night when I was asleep
I heard a funny noise
a voice that I knew
it was the old general
the old general who came back
who came back like a ghost to old haunts
with an old major
and they thought that I was asleep
and they spoke very softly.
Enough enough rice in the water
we want to feast on the beast
just put something in his oats
some gramophone needles.
My blood ran cold
like that of a wooden horse
and leaving the stable
I fled into the woods.

Now the war is over
and the old general is dead
dead in his bed
dead from his good death
but I am alive and that's the main thing
good evening
good night
bon appetit, General.

WHALE FISHING

Let's go whale fishing, let's go whale fishing,
Said the father in a furious voice
To his son Prosper, lying under the wardrobe,
Let's go whale fishing, let's go whale fishing,
You don't want to go,
And why not then?
And why should I go to fish for an animal
That has done nothing to me, papa,
Go on, go fish for it yourself,
Since you enjoy it,
I would rather stay at home with my poor mother
And cousin Gaston.
So the father goes off all by himself on his whaling ship
On the stormy sea...
There's the father on the waves,
There's the son waving him off,
There's the angry whale,
And there's cousin Gaston upsetting the soup tureen
The tureen full of broth.
The sea was bad,
The soup was good.
And there's Prosper on his chair being sorry:
I didn't go fishing for whales,
And why didn't I go anyway?
Maybe we would have caught something,
Then I could have eaten it.
But the door is opening, and dripping with water
The father appears out of breath,
Carrying the whale on his back.
He throws the animal on the table, a fine whale with blue eyes,
An unusual creature,
And says in a pitiful voice:
Hurry with jointing it,
I'm hungry, I'm thirsty, I want to eat.
But Prosper gets up,
Looking his father in the whites of his eyes

In the whites of his father's blue eyes
Blue like those of the blue-eyed whale:
And why would I chop up a poor creature who's done nothing to me?
I don't care, I renounce my share.
Then he throws the knife on the floor,
But the whale snatches it up, and throwing itself on the father
It stabs him through and through.
Oh, oh, says cousin Gaston,
That reminds me of the hunt, the butterfly hunt
And so
So Prosper prepares the announcements,
The mother goes into mourning for her poor husband
And the whale, a tear in his eye, contemplates the wrecked home.
Suddenly it cries:
And why have I killed this poor idiot,
Now the others are going to chase me by outboard motor
And then they are going to exterminate all my little family.
Then, bursting out with a disturbing laugh,
It makes for the door and says
To the widow in passing:
Madame, if anyone comes to ask for me,
Be so kind as to reply:
The whale has gone out,
Sit down,
Wait there,
It will probably be back in about fifteen years...

FOR YOU MY LOVE

I went to the bird market
And I bought birds
For you
my love
I went to the flower market
And I bought flowers
For you
my love
I went to the scrap-iron market
And I bought chains
Heavy chains
For you
my love
And then I went to the slave market
And I looked for you
But I didn't find you
my love

EVENTS

A swallow flies in the sky
flies toward its nest
its nest where there are little ones
she's taking them a parasol
some worms some mud some dandelions
lots of things to keep the children amused
in the house where the nest is
a sick young man is gradually dying in his bed
in his bed
on the pavement in front of the door
there is a guy who's drunk and talking nonsense
behind the door a boy kisses a girl
a little farther at the end of the street
a homosexual looks at another homosexual
and waves him good-bye
one of the two cries
the other pretends to
he has a small suitcase
he turns the corner of the street
and as soon as he is alone he smiles
the swallow flies by again in the sky
and the homosexual sees it
hey, a swallow...
and he goes on his way
in his bed the sick young man dies
the swallow goes past the window
looks through the pane
hey, a dead man...
it flies up to the next floor
and sees through the window glass
a murderer with his head in his hands
the victim is stashed in a corner
curled up
Another dead person, says the swallow...
the murderer with his head in his hands
wonders how he's going to get out of there

he gets up and takes out a cigarette
and sits down again
the swallow sees him
in its beak it holds a match
it knocks on the windowpane with its beak
the murderer opens the window
takes the match
Thanks, swallow...
and he lights his cigarette
You're very welcome, says the swallow
don't mention it
and it flies off swiftly...
the murderer closes the window again
sits down on a chair and smokes
the victim gets up and says
It's boring to be dead
you get really cold
Smoke this and it'll warm you up
the murderer gives her the cigarette
and the victim says Thank you very much
Don't mention it says the murderer
I owe you that much
he takes his hat he puts it on his head
and he goes away
he walks down the street
suddenly he stops
he thinks of a woman he loved very much
it's because of her that he killed
he doesn't love her any more
but he never dared tell her
he doesn't want to trouble her
now and then he kills somebody for her
for that woman
that pleases her so much
he would die rather than to make her suffer
the murderer doesn't mind suffering
but when other people suffer
he goes wild

nuts
bananas
beside himself
he does anything anywhere any time
and then afterwards he hops it
each to his own job
some kill
others get killed
everybody has to live
if you call that living
the murderer spoke out loud
and the guy who shouts to him
is sitting on the pavement
he's out of work
he stays there the whole day
sitting on the walkway
he waits for things to change
you know where I've come from the murderer says to him
the other man shakes his head
I have just killed somebody
Everybody has to die
replies the unemployed man
and suddenly point blank
Do you have news?
News of what?
News of the world
news of the world... it seems that it's going to change
life is going to become very fine
every day we'll be able to eat
there will be a lot of sunlight
all men will be life size
and no one will be humiliated
but here comes the swallow again
the murderer goes away
the unemployed man stays there
and is quiet
he listens to the sounds
he hears footsteps

and he counts them
to pass the time mechanically
1 2 3 4 5
etc... etc...
up to one hundred... several times...
it's a man who is pacing back and forth
on the ground floor
in a room full of old paper
he has the big head of a thinker
with tortoiseshell glasses
a big head of a right-thinking reed
he paces back and forth and he is searching
he is searching for something that will make him become someone
and when somebody knocks at his door he says
I'm not here to anyone
he is searching
he is searching for something that will make him become someone
the whole world could go and knock at his door
the whole world could be rolling around on his doormat
and moaning
and weeping
and begging
asking for something to drink
something to drink or eat
and he wouldn't open the door...
he is searching
he is searching for the excellent machine for weighing scales
when he finds
the excellent machine for weighing scales
he will be the most famous man in his country
the king of weights and measures
of weights and measures in France
and inside he utters little cries
hurray for papa
hurray for me
vive la France
suddenly he stubs his toe on the foot of the bed
the foot of a bed is hard

harder than the foot of a genius
and so the thinking reed is on the carpet
rocking his poor painful foot
outside the unemployed man nods his head
his poor head rocked by insomnia
near him a taxi stops
some human beings get out they are in mourning
and in tears and in their thirties
one of them pays the driver
the driver goes away
with his taxi
another human calls him gives him an address and gets in
the taxi drives off again 25 rue de Châteaudun
the driver has the address in his memory
he keeps it just as long as he needs to
but all the same it's a funny job...
and when he has a fever
when he is tight when he is in bed at night
thousands and thousands of addresses
arrive at top speed and slug it out in his memory
he has a head like a phone directory
like a map
then he takes this head in his hands
with the same gesture as the murderer
and he moans softly
222 rue de Vaugirard
33 rue de Ménilmontant
Grand Palace
St. Lazare Station
and the Last-of-the-Mohicans Street
it's crazy what man invents
to hurt man
and as all that happens quietly
the man believes he's living and yet he is already almost dead
and for a very long time
he comes and goes in depressing surroundings
the colour of family life
the colour of New Year's Day

with the portrait of the grandmother
of the grandfather and Uncle Ferdinand
the one whose ears stank so
and who had only one tooth left
the man strolls in a graveyard
and takes his gloom out for a walk on a leash
he doesn't dare say anything
he doesn't dare do anything
he is anxious for it to be all over
so when war comes
he is all ready to be a stiff
and the one who is killed
once his terror has passed
he says whew and Thank you
that's a relief
....
so the murdered man curls up
and bathing in his blood
he is very calm
and that is pleasant to see
this dead body tidied away in a corner
in these neat little lodgings
there is a silence of death
You'd think you were in a church says a fly coming in
it's touching
and all the assembled flies produce a pious buzzing
then they go toward the pool
the big pool of blood
but the senior fly tells them
Stop there, my children
let us give thanks to the god of the flies for this surprise banquet
and without one false note all the flies intone grace
the swallow passes and frowns
it detests these affectations
the flies are devout
the swallow is an atheist
it is alive
it is beautiful

it flies fast
there is a God for flies
a God for moths
for swallows there is no God
they don't need one...
the swallow continues on its way and sees
through the net curtains of another window
the whole family sitting around the dead young man
they have come in a taxi
in tears in mourning and in a jiffy
they hold a wake for the dead man
they stay there
if the family didn't stay there
the dead man would perhaps run off
or maybe another family would come
and grab him
when you have a dead man you hang onto him
and when you don't have one you wish you had one
People are so mean
right Uncle Gratien
Who are you saying that to
people are jealous
they would take our dead person from us
our own dead person
they would weep in place of us
that would be out of place
and each one in the mirror-fronted wardrobe
each watches himself cry...
an unemployed worker sitting on the pavement
a taxi on a boulevard
a dead person
another dead person
a murderer
a watering can
a swallow that comes and goes
in the sky-coloured sky
a big cloud finally bursts
the hail...

hailstones as big as a fist
everyone exhales
Whew
you can't let it get you down
you have to bear up
eat
the flies lap
the young swallows eat the dandelion
the family the sausage
the murderer a bunch of radishes
the taxi driver at the meeting place for drivers
rue de Tolbiac
eats an escalope of horsemeat
everyone eats except dead people
everyone eats
homosexuals... swallows...
giraffes... colonels...
everyone eats
except the unemployed man
the unemployed man who doesn't eat because he has nothing to ea
he is sitting on the pavement
he is very tired
in the time that he has been waiting for things to change
he begins to get fed up
suddenly he gets up
suddenly he goes away
in search of the others
the others
the others who don't eat because they have nothing to eat
the others so tired
the others sitting on pavements
and who are waiting
who are waiting for things to change and who are fed up
and who are going off in search of others
all the others
all the others who are so tired
tired of waiting
tired...

Look says the swallow to its young
there are thousands of them
and the little ones stick their heads out of the nest
and watch the men walk
If they stick together
they will eat
says the swallow
but if they break up they will die
Stay together poor people
stay united
cry the young swallows
stay together poor people
stay united
cry the little ones
some men hear them
salute with their fists
and smile.

1937

HAMLET AT SCHOOL

The Teacher: Hamlet!

Hamlet *(startled)*: What?... Eh? Excuse me... What's happening?... What's going on?... What is it?

The Teacher *(annoyed)*: You can't just say 'here' like normal people? Oh no, you're in a world of your own again.

Hamlet: To be or not to be in a world of my own!

The Teacher: That will do. Stop clowning around. Now conjugate the verb 'to be' like normal people, that's all I ask of you.

Hamlet: At være...

The Teacher: Not in Danish! Just in English, please, like normal people.

Hamlet: All right, sir. *(He conjugates)*
I am or I am not
You are or you are not
He is or he is not
We are or we are not...

The Teacher *(extremely annoyed)*: You're the one who is not... all there, my poor friend!

Hamlet: That's quite right, Sir.
I am all there or I am not
And in the end, you know, on reflection
To be all there or not to be all there
That is perhaps also the question.

PATER NOSTER

Our Father who art in Heaven
Stay there
And we will stay on Earth
Which is sometimes so lovely
With its mysteries of New York
And then its mysteries of Paris
Which are easily worth the one of the Trinity
With its little Ourcq Canal
Its Great Wall of China
Its Morlaix River
Its Blackpool Rock
With its Pacific Ocean
And its two fountains in the Tuileries
With its good kids and its bad guys
With all the wonders of the world
Which are there
Just there on the Earth
Given to everybody
Scattered about
Themselves filled with wonder at being such wonders
And which don't dare admit it
Like a pretty nude girl who doesn't dare show herself
With the terrible disasters of the world
Which are legion
With their legionnaires
With their torturers
With the masters of this world
The masters with their pastors, their traitors and their haters
With the seasons
With the years
With the pretty girls and with the bloody old fools
With the straw of misery rotting in the steel of the cannons.

THE DUNCE

He says no with his head
but he says yes with his heart
he says yes to what he loves
he says no to the teacher
he is on his feet
he is questioned
and all the problems are put to him
suddenly he laughs hysterically
and he erases everything
the words and the numbers
the names and dates
the phrases and the traps
and in spite of the teacher's threats
to the jeers of the child prodigies
with multicoloured chalk
on the blackboard of misery
he draws the face of happiness

THE RETURN HOME

A Breton returns to his native region
After having done several shady things
He walks past the factories in Douarnenez
He recognizes nobody
Nobody recognizes him
He is very sad.
He goes into a crêpe shop to eat some crêpes
But he can't eat any
There's something that keeps them from going down
He pays
He leaves
He lights a cigarette
But he can't smoke it.
There is something
Something in his head
Something bad
He gets sadder and sadder
And suddenly he begins to remember:
When he was little somebody told him
"You'll end up on the scaffold"
And for years
He never dared do anything
Not even cross the street
Not even get on a boat
Absolutely nothing at all.
He remembers.
The one who had predicted it all is Uncle Grésillard
Uncle Grésillard who brings sorrow to everybody
The swine!
And the Breton thinks of his sister
Who works in Vaugirard
Of his brother who was killed in the war
He thinks of all the things he's seen
All the things he's done.
Sadness clings to him
He tries once again

To light a cigarette
But he doesn't feel like smoking
Then he decides to go see Uncle Grésillard.
He goes to his house
He opens the door
His uncle doesn't recognize him
But he recognizes his uncle
And he says to him:
"Hello, Uncle Grésillard"
And then he wrings his neck.
And he ends up on the scaffold in Quimper
After having eaten two dozen crêpes
And smoked a cigarette.

THE CONCERT WAS NOT A SUCCESS

Companions of bad days
I wish you a good night
And I'm going away.
The takings have been bad
It's my fault
I was wrong about everything
I should have listened to you
I should have played the poodle
It's pleasing music
But I did it my own way
And then I got nervous.
When you play the wire-haired dog
You have to be careful with your bow
People don't come to the concert
To hear howling at the moon
And this song of the dog pound
Has done us the greatest harm.
Companions of the bad days
I wish you a good night
Sleep
Dream
I'm taking my cap
And then two or three cigarettes in the packet
And I'm going away...
Companions of the bad days
Think of me sometimes
Later...
When you wake up
Think of the one who plays the seal and the smoked salmon
Somewhere...
In the evening
At the seaside
And who then goes round with the hat
To buy something to eat
And something to drink...
Companions of the bad days

I wish you a good night...
Sleep
Dream
I'm leaving.

DAYS OF DREGS AND THORNS

Be forewarned old men
be forewarned heads of families
the time when you gave your sons to your country
as one gives bread to pigeons
that time will never return
make the best of it
it's over
the days of wine and roses will never return
nor the days of dregs and thorns
it's useless to moan about it
go to sleep instead
you are overcome with sleep
your shroud is freshly ironed
the sandman is on his way
prepare your chin straps
close your eyes
the night-soil dealer is going to take you away
the three musketeers are finished
this is the day of the sewermen

When with a nice smile in the metro
you asked us politely
comma, open quotes
get out at the next stop
young man
it was the war you were talking about
but you're not giving us that old patriotic crap any more

no, Captain
no Monsieur Bloggs
no papa
no mama
we will not get off at the next stop
or we'll knock you off before
you will be thrown out the door
it's more convenient than the cemetery

it's more amusing
it's faster
it's cheaper

When you drew straws
it was always the cabin boy who got eaten
but the time of jolly shipwrecks is past
when the admirals fall into the sea
don't count on us to throw them a buoy
unless it's made of stone
or a flatiron
you have to make the best of it
the time of the aged old men is finished

When you came back from the military parade
with your children on your shoulders
you were drunk without having drunk anything
and your spinal cord
was playing the proud fool
in front of the Pépinière barracks
you were right in there behind the mane
when the fine mounted dragoons rode past
and the military music
excited you from head to foot
excited you
and the children that you were carrying on your shoulders
you let them slip into the tricolour mud
into the potters' field
and your shoulders are stooped
youth must indeed pass away
you have let it die

Honourable and highly esteemed men
in your headquarters
you hold a meeting of the minds
you exchange congratulations
and coagulations
alas alas dear Monsieur Babylas

I had three sons and I gave them
to my country
alas alas dear Monsieur of my two
I gave only two of them
one does what one can
it's just that we...
do you always have sore knees
and tears in your eyes
the runny nose of grief
crêpe on your hat
your feet nice and warm
the funeral wreaths
and garlic in the pot roast
you remember before the war
the absinthe spoons the horse trams
the hairpins
the torchlight tattoos
oh how fine it was
those were the days
Shut up old men
stop moving your dead tongues
between your fake ivory teeth
the days of hair trams
the days of horse pins
those days will never return
about face march
muster your old bones
the police van
the hearse of the rich has moved forward
son of St. Louis ascend to heaven
the performance is over
all this lovely world will be found again up above
near the God of the cops
in the yard of the great police cell

Back grandfather
back father and mother
back grandparents

back old soldiers
back old chaplains
back old chaps
the performance is over
now for the young
the show is about to begin.

1936

SONG OF THE SNAILS GOING TO A FUNERAL

Two snails go off
To the funeral of a dead leaf
They have black shells
Some crêpe around their horns
They go away in the evening
On a very beautiful autumn evening
Unfortunately when they get there
It's already spring
The leaves that were dead
Have all come back to life
And the two snails
Are very disappointed
But here comes the sun
The sun who says to them
Please by all means
Sit down
Have a glass of beer
If it takes your fancy
Why not take
The bus to Paris
It leaves this evening
You'll see a bit of the world
But don't go into mourning
I'm telling you
That darkens the white of the eye
And so it is unbecoming
Stories about coffins
Are sad and not much fun
Put on your colours again
The colours of life
Then all the animals
The trees and the plants
Begin to sing
To sing at the tops of their voices
The true living song
The song of summer

And all the world of drinking
All the world of clinking glasses
It's a very lovely evening
A lovely summer evening
And the two snails
Go back home
They go away very touched
They go away very happy
As they have drunk a lot
They stagger a tiny bit
But high up there in the sky
The moon watches over them.

INTO MY HOUSE

Into my house you will come
Except that it's not my house
I don't know whose it is
I just walked in one day
Nobody was there
Only some red peppers hung up on the white wall
I stayed in that house for a long time
Nobody came
But every day and every day
I waited for you

I didn't do anything
I mean anything serious
Sometimes in the morning
I made animal noises
I bawled like a jackass
With all my strength
And that pleased me
And then I played with my feet
Feet are very intelligent
They take you very far
When you want to go very far
And then when you don't want to go out
They stay in and keep you company
And when there's music they dance
You can't dance without them
You have to be as stupid as people so often are
To say things as stupid
As stupid as his feet happy as a lark
The lark isn't happy
It is only happy when it's happy
And sad when it's sad or neither happy nor sad
Does anyone know what a lark is
Besides it isn't really called that
It is man who has called this bird that
Lark lark lark lark

How odd names are
Martin Hugo had Victor for a first name
Bonaparte had Napoleon for a first name
Why like that and not like this
A herd of bonapartes goes past in the desert
The emperor is called Dromedary
He has a cash horse and a race register
In the distance a man gallops who has only three first names
He is called Tim-Tam-Tom and doesn't have a last name
A bit farther yet there is somebody or other
Much farther still there is something or other
But then what difference does all that make

Into my house you will come
I'm thinking of something else but I think only of that
And when you enter my house
You will take off all your clothes
And you will stand still and naked with your red mouth
Like the red peppers hung on the white wall
And then you will lie down and I will lie down near you
There we are
Into my house which isn't my house you will come.

A FAMILY MATTER

The mother does her knitting
The son makes war
The mother finds this quite natural
And the father, what does the father do?
He does business
His wife does her knitting
His son makes war
He does business
The father finds that quite natural
And the son and the son
What does the son think?
He thinks nothing absolutely nothing
His mother does knitting his father business and he goes to war
When he has finished the war
He will do business with his father
War goes on the mother goes on knitting
The father goes on doing business
The son is killed he no longer goes on
The father and the mother go to the graveyard
The father and mother find that natural
Life continues – life with knitting war business
Business war knitting war
Business business and business
Life with the graveyard.

SONG IN THE BLOOD

There are big pools of blood on the world
Where does all this spilled blood go
does the earth drink it and get drunk
if so it's a funny kind of booze-up
so sensible... so monotonous...
No, the earth doesn't get drunk
the earth doesn't stagger when it turns
it drives its little car smoothly its four seasons
the rain... the snow...
the hail... the fine weather
it is never drunk
it barely allows itself now and then
a miserable little volcano
The earth turns
it turns with its trees... its gardens... its houses...
it turns with its big pools of blood
and every living thing turns with it and bleeds...
The earth
doesn't give a toss
it turns and all the living things begin to howl
it doesn't give a toss
it turns
it keeps turning
and the blood keeps flowing...
Where does all this spilled blood go
the blood of murders... the blood of wars...
the blood of misery...
and the blood of men tortured in prisons...
the blood of children calmly tortured by their mama and papa...
And the blood of men who bleed from the head
in the padded cells...
and the blood of the roofer
when the roofer slips and falls off the roof
And the blood that comes flowing in great torrents
with the newborn... with the new child...
the mother screaming... the child crying...

the blood flows... the earth turns
the earth keeps turning
the blood keeps flowing
Where does all this spilled blood go
the blood of those clubbed to death... of those humiliated...
of the suicides... of those shot... of those sentenced to death...
and the blood of those who up and die... by accident
In the street a living person walks by
with all his blood inside
suddenly he drops dead
and all his blood is outside
and the other living people make the blood disappear
they take the body away
but the blood is stubborn
and just where the dead man was
much later all black
a little blood still spreads...
coagulated blood
rust of life rust of bodies
blood curdled like milk
like milk when it turns
when it turns like the earth
like the turning earth
with its milk... with its cows...
with its living people... with its dead people
the turning earth with its trees... its living things... its houses
the turning earth with the weddings...
the funerals...
the shellfish...
the armies...
the earth that turns and turns
with its great floods of blood.

1936

WASH DAY

Oh the terrible and surprising smell of dying flesh
it's summer and yet the leaves of the trees in the garden
fall and die as though it were autumn...
this smell comes from the house
where Monsieur Edmond lives
head of the family
head of an office
it's wash day
and it's the smell of the family
and the head of the family
head of an office
in his house in the main town of the district
comes and goes around the family tub
and repeats his favourite formula
Wash your dirty linen at home
and the whole family clucks with horror
with shame
boil and brush and rub and brush
the cat would really like to go away
all that makes it sick at heart
disheartens the little pet cat
but the door is padlocked shut
so the poor little cat sicks up
the poor little scrap of heart
that it had eaten the day before
some old wallets float in the water of the tub
and then scapulars... sling bandages...
nightcaps... police caps...
insurance policies... account books
love letters dealing with money
anonymous letters dealing with love
a rosette of the Legion of Honour
old bits of earplugs
ribbons
a cassock
a pair of long johns

a wedding dress
a fig leaf
a nurse's blouse
a cavalry officer's uniform
swaddling clothes
plaster pants
smarty pants...
suddenly long sobs
and the little cat puts its paws over its ears
so as not to hear this noise
because it loves the girl
and she's the one who screams
she's the one they're after
it's the young girl of the house
she is naked... she screams... she cries...
and with a blow of a scrubbing brush on the head
the father brings her back to her senses
she has a stain
the young girl of the house
and all the family plunge her into the water
and plunge her again
she bleeds
she howls
but she won't say the name...
and the father howls too
All this mustn't leave here
All this must stay just among us
says the mother
and the sons the cousins the little brats
shout too
and the parrot on its perch
also repeats
All this mustn't leave here
family honour
father's honour
son's honour
honour of the Holy Ghost parrot
the daughter of the house is pregnant

the newborn must not
leave here
nobody knows the father's name
in the name of the father and the son
in the name of the above-mentioned Holy-Ghost parrot
All this mustn't leave here...
with a weird expression on her face
the old grandmother seated on the edge of the tub
plaits a crown of artificial flowers
for the natural child...
and the daughter is trampled
the barefoot family
trample trample and trample
it's the grape harvest of the family
the harvest of honour
the daughter of the house dies
in the end...
at the surface
soap bubbles burst
white bubbles
pale bubbles
the colour of Mary's baby
and on a piece of soap
a crab louse escapes with its little ones
the clock strikes one-thirty
and the head of the family and the office
puts his headgear on his head
and goes away
crosses the square of the main town of the region
and returns the greeting to his deputy
who greets him...
the feet of the head of the family are red
but his shoes are well polished

It is better to provoke envy than pity.

THIS LOVE

This love
So violent
So fragile
So tender
So hopeless
This love
Fine as the day
And as bad as the weather
When the weather is bad
This love so true
This love so fine
So happy
So joyous
And so pathetic
Trembling with fear like a child in the dark
And so sure of itself
Like a calm man in the middle of the night
This love that frightened others
That made them talk
That made them turn pale
This watched-for love
Because we watched out for it
Hunted wounded trampled finished off denied forgotten
Because we have hunted wounded trampled finished off
                              denied forgotten it
This unimpaired love
Still so alive
And all sunny
It's yours
It's mine
The one that was
This thing that's always new
And that hasn't changed
As true as a plant
As quivering as a bird
As hot as alive as the summer

We can both
Go and come back
We can forget
And then go back to sleep
Wake up suffer grow old
Go to sleep again
Dream of death
Wake up, smile and laugh
And grow young again
Our love stays there
As stubborn as a mule
As alive as desire
As cruel as memory
As foolish as regrets
As tender as a recollection
As cold as marble
As fine as the day
As fragile as a child
It looks at us, smiling,
And it speaks to us without saying anything
And I listen trembling
And I cry out
I cry out for you
I cry out for myself
I beg it
For you for me and for all those who love each other
And who have loved each other
Yes I cry out to it
For you for me and for all the others
Who I don't know
Stay there
There where you are
There where you used to be
Stay there
Don't budge
Don't go away
We who loved each other
We have forgotten you

Don't forget us
We had only you on earth
Don't let us become cold
Always much farther away
And no matter where
Give us a sign of life
Much later at the corner of a grove
In the forest of memory
Spring up suddenly
Hold your hand out to us
And save us.

THE MUSICIANS

I play the piano, myself,
said the one
I play the violin
said the other
I the harp I the banjo
I the cello
I the Breton bagpipe... I the flute
and I the rattle.
And everybody talked talked
talked about what they played.
Nobody was listening to the music
everybody was talking
talking talking
nobody played
but in a corner a man was keeping quiet:
"And what instrument do you play, Monsieur,
you who are keeping quiet and not saying anything?"
the musicians asked him.
"I play the base and vile
and I also bring the knife into play."
says the man who up until then
had said absolutely nothing
and then he advanced with the knife in his hand
and he killed all the musicians
and he played the base and vile
and his music was so true
and so lively and so pretty
that the little daughter of the host
comes out from under the piano
where she had been lying asleep from boredom
and she says:
"I played with a hoop
with a ball I played going hunting
I played hopscotch
I played with a bucket
I played with a spade

I played mummies and daddies
I played tag
I played with my dolls
I played with a parasol
I played with my little brother
with my little sister
I played cops
and robbers
but it's over over over
I want to play assassin
I want to play the base and vile."
And the man took the little girl by the hand
and they went off into the towns
into the houses into the gardens
and then they killed as many people as possible
after which they got married
and they had lots of children.
But
the eldest learned the piano
the second the violin
the third the harp
the fourth the rattle
the fifth the cello
and then they began to talk talk talk
talk talk talk
the music was no longer heard
and everything had to begin all over again!

PAGE OF WRITING

Two and two four
four and four eight
eight and eight equals sixteen...
Repeat! says the teacher
Two and two four
four and four eight
eight and eight equals sixteen.
But there goes the lyre bird
flying in the sky
the child sees it
the child hears it
the child calls out to it:
Save me
play with me
bird!
So the bird comes down
and plays with the child
Two plus two four...
Repeat! says the teacher
and the child plays
the bird plays with him...
Four plus four eight
eight plus eight equals sixteen
and sixteen plus sixteen, what does that equal?
Sixteen plus sixteen doesn't equal anything
and especially not thirty-two
in any case
and they go away.
And the child hid the bird
in his desk
and all the children
hear its song
and all the children
hear the music
and eight and eight go away in their turn
and four and four and two and two

in their turn clear off
and one plus one equals neither one nor two
one by one they go away too.
And the lyre bird plays
and the child sings
and the teacher shouts:
Would you stop that fooling around!
But all the other children
listen to the music
and the walls of the classroom
quietly fall away.
And the window panes turn back into sand
the ink turns back into water
the desks turn back into trees
the chalk turns back into cliffs
the quill holder turns back into a bird.

BREAKFAST

He put the coffee
In the cup
He put the milk
In the cup of coffee
He put the sugar
In the milky coffee
With the coffee spoon
He stirred
He drank the milky coffee
And he put the cup back down
Without speaking to me
He lit
A cigarette
He blew rings
With the smoke
He put the ashes
In the ashtray
Without speaking to me
Without looking at me
He stood up
He put
His hat on his head
He put on
His raincoat
Because it was raining
And he left
In the rain
Without a word
Without looking at me
And I put
My head in my hands
And I wept.

GIRL OF STEEL

Girl of steel I didn't love anyone in the world
I didn't love anyone except the man I loved
My lover my lover the one who attracted me
Now everything has changed is it he who stopped loving me
My lover who stopped attracting me is it me?
I don't know and then what difference does all that make?
Now I'm lying on the straw damp with love
All alone with all the others all alone in despair
Girl of tin rusty girl
O my lover my lover dead or alive
I want you to remember the old days
My lover the man who loved me and who I loved.

DESPAIR IS SITTING ON A BENCH

In a square on a bench
There is a man who calls to you when you go by
He has pince-nez an old grey suit
He smokes a small cigar he is sitting
And he calls to you when you go by
Or he simply makes a sign to you
You mustn't look at him
You mustn't listen to him
You must go on past
Pretend you didn't see him
Pretend you didn't hear him
You have to go on past, walk faster
If you look at him
If you listen to him
He makes a sign to you and nobody, nothing
Can prevent you from going to sit down near him
So he looks at you and smiles
And you suffer horribly
And the man goes on smiling
And you smile with the same smile
Exactly
The more you smile the more you suffer
Horribly
The more you suffer the more you smile
Irremediably
And you stay there
Sitting rooted to the spot
Smiling on the bench
Children play near you
Passers-by pass by
Calmly
Birds fly away
Leaving one tree
For another
And you stay there
On the bench

And you know you know
That you will never again play
Like those children
You know that you will never again pass by
Calmly
Like those passers-by
That you will never again take flight
Leaving one tree for another
Like those birds.

TO MAKE A PORTRAIT OF A BIRD

To Elsa Henriquez

First paint a cage
with an open door
then paint
something pretty
something simple
something fine
something useful
for the bird
next place the canvas against a tree
in a garden
in a wood
or in a forest
hide behind the tree
without saying anything
without moving...
Sometimes the bird comes quickly
but it can just as well take long years
to make up its mind
Don't lose heart
wait
wait for years if necessary
whether the bird comes quickly or slowly
having no connection
with the success of the picture
When the bird comes
if it comes
keep very still
wait for the bird to go into the cage
and when it has gone in
gently close the door with the brush
then
erase all the bars one by one
taking care not to touch any of the bird's feathers
Next make the portrait of the tree
choosing the most beautiful of its branches

for the bird
also paint the green foliage and the coolness of the wind
the dust motes in the sunlight
and the sound of the animals in the grass in the summer heat
and then wait for the bird to decide to sing
If the bird doesn't sing
it's a bad sign
a sign that the picture is bad
but if it sings it's a good sign
a sign that you can sign
Then you very gently pull out
one of the bird's feathers
and you write your name in a corner of the picture.

THE SUPPER

They're sitting around the table
They're not eating a thing
They've got a lot on their plates
And their plates are all standing
Straight up behind their heads.

GRAND FAMILIES

Louis I
Louis II
Louis III
Louis IV
Louis V
Louis VI
Louis VII
Louis VIII
Louis IX
Louis X (the Quarrelsome)
Louis XI
Louis XII
Louis XIII
Louis XIV
Louis XV
Louis XVI
Louis XVIII
and nobody, nothing more...
what's with those people
who can't bloody well even
count up to twenty?

THE SCHOOL OF FINE ARTS

In a box of woven straw
The father chooses a little ball of paper
And he tosses it
Into the basin
In front of his fascinated children
Then there appears
Multicoloured
The big Japanese flower
The instantaneous water lily
And the children are quiet
Astonished
Later in their memories
This flower can never wilt
This sudden flower
Made for them
On the spot
In front of them.

SACRED SCRIPTURES

To Elizabeth and Darcy
to the mortise and the tenon
to the cock and the bull
to the mote and to the beam
to the top and the bottom of the barrel
to St. Leonard and to Hastings
to the one and to the two
to the spider and to the ant
to the zig and to the zag
to your health and to mine
to the good and to the bad
to God and to the Devil
to Laurel and to Hardy.

God is a large rabbit
He lives higher than the earth
way high up in the sky
in his big cloudy burrow.
The devil is a large red hare
With a grey rifle
to shoot in the gloom of night
but God is a big rabbit
he has the ear of the world
he knows what's what
once he had a big son
a happy rabbit
and he sent him down to earth
to save the rabbits down below
and his son was quickly dispatched
and he was called jugged hare.
Of course he had some quite bad times
and then he had another go at it
he put his bones back in their place
the kidneys the saddle the head and everything
and he made a tremendous leap
and there he is now tough rabbit

hopping in heaven
to the left and the right
of the great almighty rabbit.
And the devil shoots in the dark
and comes back every night empty handed
he hasn't been able
to bag something for his table
and he flies into a towering rage
he tears his cap off his head
and he stamps in the dust
and afterwards it hasn't got him anywhere
and he has to wear
his Sunday hat
on all the days that the rabbit makes.
But his Sunday hat
is a ghost of a rabbit
a will-o-the-wisp of the factories
and he clowns around
that's why the devil
never has his hat on his head
not even on holidays
but beside his head
above his head
or even like this behind his head
yes
exactly ten or fifteen centimetres
behind his head
and he gets migraines all the time
from gusts of wind
and inflammations in his ears.
When he encounters God
he is very worried
because he ought to doff his hat to him
it's the correct thing
because God is the founder
of heaven and earth
he alone is the inventor
of flint for cigarette lighters

and God says to him
Please my friend keep your hat on
but the devil cannot
put yourself in his place
since his hat doesn't stay put
he realises
that he is slightly ridiculous
and he goes running back home
he lights a big fire crying all the while
and he looks at himself in his wardrobe mirror
making faces
and then he throws the wardrobe on the fire
and when the wardrobe begins to pop
to crackle to creak
he suddenly becomes very happy
and he lies down on the fire
with a big white flame
as a pillow
and he purrs softly
like the fire
like cats when they're happy
and he dreams of the tricks
that he is going to play on God.

God is also a pawnbroker
an old money-lender
he hides in a crummy little dump
over his pawnshop
and he lends money at a high rate of interest by the week
by the month by the century and by eternity
and those who come back down with a little money
down below in the valley the devil waits for them
he pinches their dough off them
he works them over
and goes off singing a jaunty tune.
God is also a great traveller
and when he travels
there's no way to make him stay put

he sets up shop all over the place
and he goes down into all the hotels at once
at those times
all travellers walk on foot
and bed down out-of-doors
and the devil goes by
and shouts
Pillows blankets
and they all call to him
Hey! Here!
but he's just saying that
just to get their goat all the more
he has better things to do
than to really care about those people
he's only mildly pleased
because they're getting cold.

God is also a big Christmas turkey
who has himself eaten by the rich
to wish his son a happy birthday.
Then elbows on the holy table
the Devil looks God in the face
with a lop-sided smile
and he thumbs his nose at the angels and God is really pissed off.

THE BROKEN MIRROR

The little man who sang constantly
the little man who danced in my head
the little man of youth
broke his shoelace
and all the stalls of the fair
suddenly collapsed
and in the silence of this fair
in the desert of this fair
I heard your happy voice
your torn and fragile voice
childish and distressed
coming from far away and calling me
and I put my hand on my heart
where there moved
blood-soaked
the seven icy splinters of your star-cracked laugh.

TAKING LIBERTIES

I put my cap in the cage
and went out with the bird on my head.
So
we've stopped saluting have we
asked the major
Right
said the bird
we've stopped saluting
Oh I see
excuse me I thought we still did it
said the major
That's quite all right anyone can make a mistake
said the bird.

THE EXAMPLE OF BIRDS

I learned very late in life to love birds
I am rather sorry about that
but now everything is straightened out
we see eye to eye
they don't concern themselves with me
I don't concern myself with them
I look at them
I let them alone
all the birds are doing their best
they set an example
not an example like for example Monsieur Glacis who
        conducted himself remarkably courageously during
        the war or the example of little Paul who was so
        poor and so handsome and so honest to boot and who
        later became big Paul so rich and so old so
        honourable and so horrid and so miserly and so
        charitable and so devout
or for example this old servant-woman who had an
        exemplary life and death never any arguments the
        fingernail clicking on the tooth no dispute with
        monsieur or with madame on the subject of this
        vexed question of wages
no
the birds set an example
the proper example
example of birds
example of birds
example the feathers the wings the flight of birds
example the nest the travels and the songs of birds
example the beauty of birds
example the heart of birds
the light of birds.

SONG OF THE JAILER

Where are you going fine jailer
With this blood-stained key
I am going to release the woman I love
If there is still time for it
Who I locked up
Tenderly cruelly
In the most secret place of my desire
In the most profound place of my agony
In the falsehoods of the future
In the foolishness of the promises
I want to release her
I want her to be free
And even to forget me
And even to go away
And even to come back
And to love me again
Or to love somebody else
If somebody else pleases her
And if I remain alone
And she stays away
I will keep only
I will keep always
In my two cupped hands
Until the end of my days
The softness of her breasts shaped by love.

FIRST DAY

Some white sheets in a cupboard
Some red sheets on a bed
A child in its mother
Its mother in labour
The father in the hallway
The hallway in a house
The house in the city
The city in the night
Death in a cry
And the child in life.

THE MESSAGE

The door that someone opened
The door that someone closed again
The chair where someone sat
The cat that someone stroked
The fruit that someone bit
The letter that someone read
The chair that someone knocked over
The door that someone opened
The road that someone runs down again
The woods that someone goes through
The river that someone jumps in
The hospital where someone died.

AT THE FLORIST'S

A man goes into a florist's
and chooses some flowers
the florist wraps up the flowers
the man puts his hand in his pocket
to get the money
the money to pay for the flowers
but suddenly
at the same time he puts
his hand on his heart
and he falls down

At the same time that he falls down
the money hits the floor
and then the flowers fall
at the same time as the man
at the same time as the money
and the florist stands there
with the money rolling around
with the flowers that are getting ruined
with the man who is dying
obviously all that is very sad
and the florist
has to do something
but she doesn't know what to do first
she doesn't know
where to begin

There are so many things to do
with this man who's dying
these flowers that are getting ruined
and this money
this money in circulation
that keeps going around

VINCENT'S LAMENT

to Paul Eluard

In Arles where the Rhone runs
In the unbearable light of the south
A man of phosphorus and blood
Utters a haunting wail
Like a woman giving birth
And the linen turns red
And the man runs away screaming
Pursued by the sun
A sun of a harsh yellow
At a brothel close to the Rhone
The man arrives like a Wise Man
With his absurd present
He has a blue and gentle look
The true lucid and mad look
Of those who give everything to life
Of those who aren't jealous
And shows the poor child
His ear lying in the linen
And she cries without understanding anything
Thinking of sad omens
And looks without daring to pick it up
The hideous and delicate shell
Where the moans of dead love
And the inhuman voices of art
Mingle with the murmurs of the sea
And go to die on the tiled floor
In the room where the red quilt
Of a sudden dazzling red
Mixes this very red red
Much redder than blood
Of Vincent half dead
And wise as the very image
Of misery and love
The naked ageless child all alone
Looks at poor Vincent

Struck by the lightning of his own storm
Who collapses on the tiled floor
Lying in his finest picture
And the storm goes away calmed unconcerned
And gushing in front of him his big buckets of blood
The dazzling storm of Vincent's genius
And Vincent stays there sleeping dreaming rattling
And the sun above the brothel
Like a demented orange in a nameless desert
The sun above Arles
Goes around in circles screaming.

THE GARDEN

Thousands and thousands of years
Would not be enough
To express
The little second of eternity
When you kissed me
When I kissed you
One morning in the slight winter light
In the half dark Montsouris Park in Paris
In Paris
On the Earth
The Earth which is a star.

PARIS AT NIGHT

Three matches lit one by one in the night
The first to see your whole face
The second to see your eyes
The last to see your mouth
And complete darkness to remind me of all that
As I hold you in my arms.

BARBARA

Remember Barbara
It was raining constantly in Brest that day
And you were walking along smiling
Radiant delighted dripping wet
In the rain
Remember Barbara
It was raining constantly in Brest
And I passed you in the rue de Siam
You smiled
And I smiled back
Remember Barbara
You who I didn't know
You who didn't know me
Remember
Remember that day all the same
Don't forget
A man was sheltering in a doorway
And he called your name
Barbara
And you ran toward him in the rain
Dripping wet delighted radiant
And you threw yourself into his arms
Remember that Barbara
And don't hold it against me if I call you *tu*
I say *tu* to everyone I love
Even if I have seen them only once
I say *tu* to people who love each other
Even if I don't know them
Remember Barbara
Don't forget
That wise and happy rain
On your happy face
On this happy city
This rain on the sea
On the arsenal
On the ferry to Ouessant

Oh Barbara
The sheer bloody stupidity of war
What has become of you now
Under that rain of iron
Of fire of steel of blood
And the man who held you in his arms
Lovingly
Is he dead disappeared or still alive
Oh Barbara
It is raining constantly in Brest
As it rained before
But it's not the same any more and everything is ruined
It's a rain of terrible and desolate grief
Nor is there a storm now
Of iron steel blood
Quite simply clouds
That burst like balloons
Balloons that vanish
In the water streaming on Brest
And are going to disintegrate far away
Far away very far from Brest
Of which there is nothing left.

INVENTORY

One stone
two houses
three ruins
four gravediggers
one garden
some flowers

one raccoon

one dozen oysters a lemon a loaf of bread
a ray of sunshine
a groundswell
six musicians
one door with its doormat
one man decorated with the Legion of Honour

another raccoon

a sculptor who sculpts Napoleons
the flower they call honesty
two lovers on a double bed
one tax collector a chair three turkeys
a clergyman a boil
a wasp
one floating kidney
one racing stable
one unworthy son two dominican friars three grasshoppers
                                        a jump seat
two prostitutes one Uncle Cyprian
one Mater Dolorosa three doting daddies two goats
                        belonging to Monsieur Seguin
one Louis XV heel
a Louis XVI armchair
one Henri II sideboard two Henri III sideboards three
                                Henri IV sideboards
an odd drawer

one ball of string two safety pins one elderly gentleman
one Winged Victory one bookkeeper two assistant bookkeepers
             one man of the world two surgeons three vegetarians
one cannibal
one colonial expedition a stallion a half pint of good blood
                                                    a tse-tse fly
an American-style lobster a French-style garden
two English-style apples
one lorgnette a footman an orphan an iron lung
a night to remember
a week of brotherhood
a month of Sundays
a terrible year
one minute of silence
one second of inattention
and...

five or six raccoons

one little boy going into school crying
one little boy coming out of school smiling
one ant
two flints for a cigarette lighter
seventeen elephants one examining magistrate on holiday
                                      sitting on a folding chair
one landscape painting with a lot of green grass in it
one cow
one bull
two fine love affairs three large pipe organs a veal Marengo
one sunny morning
one soda water siphon
one white wine with lemon
one Tom Thumb one pilgrimage procession a stone crucifix
                                                  a rope ladder

two hemispheres three dimensions twelve apostles a thousand
and one nights thirty-two positions six parts of the
world five cardinal points ten years of good and loyal
service seven deadly sins two fingers of the hand ten
drops before each meal thirty days in jail fifteen of
them in solitary five minute interval.

and...

several raccoons.

DO NOT...

Do not let intellectuals play with
matches
Because Gentlemen when you leave it to its own devices
The mental world Gennntlemen
Is not at all brilliant
And as soon as it is alone
It works arbitrarily
Erecting for itself
And supposedly generously in honour of the work
ers of the building trade
A self-monument
We say it again Gennnntlemen
When you leave it to its own devices
The mental world
Lies
Monumental-lie.

THE CONDUCTOR

Let's go let's go
Hurry up
Let's go let's go
Come on hurry up
There are too many passengers
Too many passengers
Hurry hurry
Some of them are forming a queue
They're everywhere
Many
All along the quay
Or in the passageways of their mothers' bellies
Let's go hurry up press on
Press on the trigger
Everyone has to live
So kill yourselves a little
Let's go let's go
Come on
Let's be serious
Give up your place
You know very well you can't stay there
For too long
There has to be room for everybody
A little tour they told you
A little turn around the world
A little tour in the world
A little tour and then you go
Let's go let's go
Hurry hurry
Be polite
Don't push.

A WASTE OF TIME

In front of the factory gate
the worker suddenly stops
the fine weather has tugged him by the sleeve
and as he turns around
and looks at the sun
all round and red up high
smiling down from its blazing sky
he winks
familiarly
Say comrade Sun
don't you think
that it's a dead loss
to give a day like this
to a boss?

PROCESSION

An old man in gold with a watch in mourning
A queen of sorrow with a man of England
And toilers of the peace with guardians of the sea
A stuffed hussar and a death's-head turkey
A coffee snake with a rattle grinder
A tightrope hunter with a head walker
A meerschaum general and a retired pipe
A little tyke in a dark suit with a gentleman in rompers
A gallows composer with a music bird
A picker-up of conscience with a prick of cigarette ends
A Wellington grinder with a duke of scissors
A little sister of Bengal with a tiger of St. Vincent de Paul
A professor of porcelain with a mender of philosophy
An inspector of the Round Table with some knights of the
                                        Paris Gas Company
A toad in exile with a Napoleon in the hole
A Winged caretaker with a cemetery Victory
A tug boat of a large family with a father of the open sea
A member of the prostate with an enlargement of the French
                                        Academy
A big diocesan horse with a grand circus bishop
A conductor under a crucifix with a choir boy in a bus
A dental urchin with a street surgeon
And the general of the oysters with an opener of Jesuits.

WEDDINGS AND BANQUETS

To William Blake

In the ruins of a cathedral
A butcher cries like a stuck pig
Because of the death of a bird
And lying on the split tombstone slabs
A fallen and cracked bell
Shows its rusty clapper
Like a fat obscene priest
Whose cassock is lifted by the wind
And in the remains of the vestry
There are three or four rascals that
Pass around the hat
On the occasion of the marriage of Heaven and Hell
It happens in England and goes down well
And also in honour of the French Revolution
And even of Louis XVI's execution
The best man is named William Blake
He is completely naked and very correct
But he keeps his hat on his head
Because the Holy Spirit is inside
It is the Holy Spirit of Contradiction
When it is asked Spirit, are you there
With a sweet smile this bird always replies
No
At the end of the wedding William Blake will make a gift of
it to the butcher
He will forget his late parrot
And he will go back to killing animals
With a heavy mallet
We are nothing like a bird
Thinks William Blake
While thinking of something else
That is of nothing but looking
At a dazzling girl invited to the wedding by whom nobody knows
And who is very beautiful there and as naked as he is without
clothes

A beauty
Thinks William a beauty with a radiant calm
As pure as red wine
And as innocent as the Spring
And he looks at her because he desires her
She looks at him too because perhaps she desires him too
Just then a large lyre bird
Arrives with its lyre
And it plays a tune of all times and all countries
And the wedding begins
The wedding properly speaking
Specifies William Blake
For there are things that are so badly expressed
And in such an improper way
Are you saying that for the hell of it
Asks an old man with a head like a prophet or a bishop
Who seems very annoyed
But William Blake is a *gentleman*
A gentle man as English people say
And he has no wish to argue with a bishop
When the marriage of Heaven and Hell takes place today
And also who knows maybe even
His own wedding
Since the pretty girl is so beautiful
And without any doubt he loves her
And perhaps she loves him too
So he contents himself with saying
To the man with a head like a bishop or prophet or a safety pin

"As the caterpillar chooses the fairest leaves to lay her eggs on,
so the priest lays his curse on the fairest joys."

And then before the music
We'll repeat it again for the hell of it
And as he said On with the music
The music comes on
And behind it the dazzling girl
Who smiles at William Blake

Because one day he also said

"Prisons are built with stones of Law, brothels
with bricks of Religion."

And she gives him her arm
And all the rest with it
And who is a happy man
It's William
William Blake.

BLOOD ORANGE

The zipper slid down your back
and all the happy storm of your loving body
in the midst of the darkness
suddenly broke out
And your dress falling on the waxed parquet
made no more sound
than an orange peel falling on the ground
But under our feet
its little pearl buttons crackled like pips
Blood orange
pretty fruit all right
the tip of your breast
has drawn a new line of good luck
on my palm with its zest
Blood orange
pretty fruit all right

Sunshine at night.

HE WOULDN'T LET ME ALONE

He wouldn't let me alone
for months days hours
and he put his hand on my breast
calling me his sweetheart
And he wrenched a promise out of me
as you wrench a flower out of the ground
And he kept this promise in his head
as you keep a flower in a greenhouse
I forgot my promise
and the flower faded at once
And his eyes started out of their sockets
he scowled at me
and he insulted me
Another man came who asked nothing of me
but he looked at me all over
I was already naked for him
from top to toes
and when he removed my clothes
I didn't resist
And I didn't know who he was.

YOUNG PEOPLE IN LOVE

Young people in love kiss standing
Against the gates of the night
And the passing passers-by point at them
But the young people in love
Are not there for anybody
And it's only their shadows
That flicker in the night
Exciting the rage of the passers-by
Their rage their scorn their laughter and their envy
The young people in love are not there for anyone
They are somewhere else much farther away than the night
Much higher than the day
In the dazzling light of their first love.

PARADE GROUNDS FOR COMPLAINT

Sleepwalker in broad daylight
I cross the parade ground
where men learn how to die
Entangled in the sheets of the dream
I stagger like a drunk
Look a ghost says the major
No
only a slacker
says the captain
In times of war his case is clear
says the lieutenant
the more so because he is not dressed correctly
For a slacker
a suit of planks
is the regulation dress
says the major
A large plank above
a large plank below
a smaller one at the foot end
a smaller one at the head end
and that's that

Excuse me
I was just passing by
I was sleeping when the bugle blew
And it was so nice in my dream
that ever since the war began
I have slept late day and night
The major says
Give him a horse an axe a magnum a flame-thrower a toothpick
                                        a screwdriver
Whatever it takes for him to do his duty on the field and on
                                        the double

I never knew how to do my duty
I never knew how to learn a lesson

But give me a horse
I'll lead it to water
Give me a magnum too
I'll drink it with friends
Give me...
but I ask nothing more of you
standard issue doesn't fit me to a tee
The killing fields are not for me

I don't want a smoking gun but a pipe
a little clay pipe
made of scorched earth
and I'm fond of it
Let me go my own way
smoking it
night and day.

Standard issue doesn't fit me to a tee
Your warpath isn't where I want to be
I smoke
my little peace pipe of clay
there's no point you getting angry
I'm not asking you for an ashtray.

PUBLIC CONFESSION

(Critical Condition)

We have mixed everything up
it's a fact
We have taken advantage of Pentecost to get hold of Easter
                eggs from St. Bartholomew's on the Christmas tree
                                of Bastille Day
The result wasn't good
The eggs were too red
The dove got away
We've mixed everything up
its a fact
The days with the years the desires with the regrets and the
                                milk with the coffee
In a month of Sundays to make it all the finer we have placed
        Friday the Thirteenth and Ash Wednesday the day of the
        death of Louis XVI the Annus Horribilis the Eleventh
        Hour and a five minute buffet stop.
And we have added without rhyme or reason without time or
        season without factories and without prisons the great
        week of forty hours and that of four Thursdays
And a minute of noise
please
One minute of cries of joy of songs of laughter and of noises
                        and of long nights for sleeping in winter with
        supplementary hours for dreaming that you are in summer and
                        of long days for making love and of rivers for
                bathing of strong sunlight for drying ourselves off
We have wasted our time
it's a fact
but it was such a bad time
We've turned the clock forward
we've torn the dead leaves from the calendar
But we've left stones unturned
it's a fact

We've only slid down the banister of the stairway
We've talked about hanging gardens
you were already on the flying fortresses
and you're going to raze a town faster than the barber's razor
                              can shave the village on a Sunday morning
Ruins while-U-wait
the dyer himself has died
How is anyone supposed to wear mourning.

                    August 1940, Jurançon.

THE RIVER

Your young breasts were shining under the moon
but he threw
the icy pebble
the cold stone of jealousy
onto the reflection
of your beauty
which was dancing naked on the river
in the splendour of the summer.

THE BETRAYED LOVERS

I gathered the corn
and you lifted the potatoes
who spilled the beans?

THE BREATHLESS TIME

Marvelling at everything never surprised by anything
a little girl sang
following the seasons following her road

When onions make me laugh
carrots will make me cry
the apple of the alphabet taught me to read
read properly

But a crank handle has unwound the Spring
and shards of ice have flown up at its face

I have too many tears to cry
they are making war on nature
I used to call the sun by its first name
and now I can't look it in the face again.

UNDER THE PLOUGHSHARE...

Under the ploughshare of your sweet steely look
my heart moved
and in this ploughed land
the flower of farewell began to shout

Today
in the same town
the town where we parted
I am the only one to see your statue
in Disappearance Place
Already thousands of days have passed
since that day when I held you last
and sometimes I look at myself in the mirror
without having the courage to shave
And that always happens on a Monday
barbers are closed on Mondays
and that upsets me
So I open the window
and I call you
and you're there
with a golden razor and a silver shaving brush
and the big bathtub of your last lover
in its forty horsepower of wind and thunder
I meet you again
and I shave as no prince has ever shaved
and I bathe at a hundred and fifty per hour
as nobody else in the world
except those who have already had a similar thing happen
has ever bathed
I don't even ask you where we're going
and it's not out of tact
but because I know for a fact
that you have no idea
And as always you ask me riddles
you ask me on what day death was born
or if life might die as suddenly as it started

you ask me why I'm laughing
and how we parted

A double-barrelled man is sitting at the wheel
the car belongs to him
he doesn't know who exactly is inside

And me with my hands full of soap
I put them over his eyes
Boo who's there
And the car lurches so much that...
But there will always be a hole in the wall of the winter to
                                see the most beautiful summer again

In the scrap iron twisted broken the spurted blood
a fire of joy broke out
And without anyone calling them
the happy memories come to reply present
and take their places again at the fireside

Time doesn't know the hour
the hour doesn't tell the time

One day a flash of passion
ran through both of us
happy scar of happiness
who can ever erase it.

NOW I'VE GROWN UP

As a child
I lived hilariously
hysterical laughter every day
really hysterical laughter
and then a sadness so sad
sometimes both at the same time
Then I thought I was in despair
Quite simply I had no hope
I had nothing but being alive
I was virginal
I was happy
and I was sad
but I never let on
I knew the gestures to stay alive
Shake the head
to say no
shake the head
to keep out other people's ideas
Shake the head to say no
and smile to say yes
yes to things and beings
to beings and to things to look at to caress
to love
to take or to leave
I was as I was
without opinions
And when I needed ideas
to keep me company
I called them
And they came
and I said yes to the ones I liked
I threw out the others

Now I've grown up
the ideas have too
but they are always big ideas
beautiful ideas
ideal ideas
And I always laugh in their faces
But they lie in wait for me
to avenge themselves
and eat me
one day when I'm very tired
But in the corner of a wood
I lie in wait for them too
and I slit their throats
I spoil their appetites.

SONG FOR YOU

To Florence

Black hair black hair
caressed by the waves
black hair black hair
ruffled by the wind
The mist of September
floats behind the trees
the sun is a green lemon
And Poverty
in its empty cart
drawn by three children who are too blond
crosses the rubble
and goes toward the sea
Black hair black hair
caressed by the waves
black hair black hair
ruffled by the wind
With its iron barrels
its debris of reinforced concrete
like a dead dog
with its paws in the air
the raft of the Admiralty
lies beached on the shingle
Black hair black hair
ruffled by the waves
black hair black hair
caressed by the wind
Sun
green lemon swept away by time
the voice of the siren
is the voice of a child.

THE VISIT TO THE MUSEUM

At the wax museum of Memory
you visit the gallery of failed projects
the corridor of half-hearted attempts
the stairway of false desires
and you fall into the trap of regrets
There
you can carve on the walls
with the little souvenir knife you bought at the entrance
the graffiti of misunderstanding
But
above the room of Wasted Advantages
his eyes blindfolded
the tightrope walker Love
walks on the taut rope of a glimpse of happiness
of happiness never forgotten
And the music of his circus
plays its scratched and worn exhausted but delighted record
and the record plays like a bleeding and sorrowing moon
radiant alive smiling sunny
amazing and amazed
Music of the people of the birds
music of the birds of the people
Visitors
don't listen to this music without hearing it
don't lend only an ear to this music
to this sound
give it your full attention
It will repay you a hundredfold
one fine day
or some other day
the music of the people of the birds of love.

SO MANY FORESTS...

So many forests uprooted from the earth
and murdered
finished off
sawed up

So many forests sacrificed for paper pulp
billions of newspapers annually drawing the attention of their
    readers to the dangers of the depletion of woods and forests.

MY LITTLE LIONESS

My little lioness
I didn't like it when you scratched me
and I threw you to the Christians
Yet I loved you very much
Please forgive me
my little lioness.

THE TENDER AND DANGEROUS FACE OF LOVE

The tender and dangerous
face of love
appeared to me one evening
after an over-long day
It was perhaps an archer
with his bow
or then again a musician
with his harp
I don't really know
I don't know anything
All I can see
Is that he wounded me
maybe with an arrow
maybe with a song
All I can see
is that he wounded me
wounded me in the heart
and for ever
Burning hot
the wound of love.

FIESTA

And the glasses were empty
and the bottle killed
And the bed was wide open
and the door closed
And all the glass stars
of happiness and of beauty
glittered in the dust
of the unswept room
And I was dead drunk
and I was on fire with joy
and you were live drunk
naked in my arms.

THE NEW SEASON

A fertile land
A good-natured moon
A hospitable sea
A smiling sun
Downstream
The girls of thin air
And all the boys of the earth
Swim in the deepest delight
Never summer never winter
Never autumn nor spring
Simply fine weather all the time
And God expelled from the earthly paradise
By these adorable children
Who don't acknowledge either Adam or Eve
God goes away to look for work in a factory
Work for him and for his serpent
But the factory isn't there any more
There is only
A fertile land
A good-natured moon
A hospitable sea
A smiling sun
And God with his reptile
Stays there
Big St. John as before
Overtaken by events.

THE CAT AND THE BIRD

A village listens heartbroken
To the song of a wounded bird
It's the only bird in the village
And it's the only cat in the village
Who half ate it
And the bird stops singing
The cat stops purring
And licking its chops
And the village gives the bird
A splendid funeral
And the cat who is invited
Walks behind the little straw coffin
Where the dead bird is laid out
Carried by a little girl
Who can't stop crying
If I had known that it would hurt you so
The cat tells her
I would have eaten it all up
And then I would have told you
That I had seen it fly away
Fly away to the other side of the world
Over there so far away
That nobody ever comes back
You would have grieved less
Just been sad and regretful

One should never do things by halves.

THE RESTAURANT BILL

The Customer: Waiter, the bill!

The Waiter: All right *(He takes out his pencil and writes.)* You had... two hardboiled eggs, one veal, peas, asparagus, one cheese with butter, one green almonds, one filter coffee, and a telephone.

The Customer: And cigarettes too!

The Waiter: *(He begins to calculate)*
Yes, right... cigarettes... so that makes...

The Customer: Don't go on, my friend, it's no use, you'll never manage it.

The Waiter: !!!

The Customer: Didn't they teach you at school that it's ma-the-ma-ti-cal-ly impossible to add unlike things?

The Waiter: !!!

The Customer: *(raising his voice)* So, anyway, who are you trying to kid?... You must be completely out of your mind even to think of trying to attempt to "add" veal to cigarettes, cigarettes to a filter coffee, filter coffee to a green almond and hardboiled eggs to peas, peas to a telephone... Why not add an order of peas to a grand officer of the Legion of Honour, while you're at it! *(He stands up.)*

No, my friend, believe me, give up now, don't wear yourself out, you'll gain nothing by it, you understand, nothing, absolutely nothing... not even the tip!

(And he leaves, taking the napkin ring with him for free.)

SONG OF THE SHOESHINE BOYS

Today the white man
Isn't astonished by anything any more
And when he tosses a miserable coin
To the black boy
The kindly Broadway shoeshine boy
He doesn't bother to see
The reflection of the sun shimmering at his feet
As he disappears
Into the Broadway crowd
His oblivious steps carry away the light
That the black boy took out of the trap
Like a true professional
The little fugitive light
That the black boy with snowy teeth
Gently tamed
With an old brush
With an old rag
With a big smile
With a little song
The song that tells the story
The story of Tom the big black man
The emperor of the shoeshine boys
In the pitch black sky of Harlem
Tom's stall is set up
Everything that sparkles in the black neighbourhood
He's the one who makes it sparkle
With his big brushes
With his old rags
With his big smile
And with his songs
He's the one who transforms to silvery white
The moon's old sandals
He's the one who shines
The patent leather shoes of the night
And who leaves in front of each door
At the big hotel of the small hours

The new shoes of the morning
And he's the one who polishes the brass
Of all the dance bands of Harlem
He's the one who sings the joy of living
The joy of making love and the joy of dancing
And then the joy of being drunk
And the joy of singing
But of the song of the Black
The white man understands nothing at all
And all he hears
Is the sound in his hand
The wretched sound of a coin
That hops without saying anything
That hops without sparkling
Sadly on one foot.

THE WONDERS OF FREEDOM

Between the teeth of a trap
The paw of a white fox
And blood on the snow
The blood of the white fox
And tracks in the snow
The tracks of the white fox
Who escapes on three legs
In the setting sun
With between his own teeth
A hare that is still alive.

AS IF BY A MIRACLE

As if by a miracle
Oranges on the branches of an orange tree
As if by a miracle
A man goes along
Putting as if by a miracle
One foot in front of the other to walk
As if by a miracle
A white stone house
Is set on the earth behind him
As if by a miracle
The man stops at the foot of the orange tree
Picks an orange peels it and eats it
Throws the peel away and spits out the pips
Quenching as if by a miracle
His great morning thirst
As if by a miracle
The man smiles
Watching the sun rising
And shining
As if by a miracle
And the dazzled man goes back into his house
And again finds as if by a miracle
His wife asleep
Amazed
To see her so young so beautiful
And as if by a miracle
Naked in the sunlight
He looks at her
And as if by a miracle she wakes up
And smiles at him
As if by a miracle he caresses her
And as if by a miracle she lets herself be caressed
Then as if by a miracle
Some birds of passage pass
Who pass just like that
As if by a miracle

Some birds of passage that are going away toward the sea
Flying very high
Over the stone house
Where the man and the woman
As if by a miracle
Are making love
Some birds of passage over the garden
Where as if by a miracle the orange tree cradles its oranges
In the morning wind
Throwing as if by a miracle its shadow on the road
On the road where a priest is going along
His nose in his breviary the breviary in his hands
And the priest treading on the orange peel thrown away by the man
Slips and falls
Like a priest who slips on an orange peel and falls on the road
One fine morning.

THE MAN WHO WAS SHOT

The flowers the gardens the fountains the smiles
And the sweetness of living
A man is there on the ground soaked in his own blood
The memories the flowers the fountains the gardens
The childhood dreams
A man is there on the ground like a bleeding parcel
The flowers the fountains the gardens the memories
And the sweetness of living
A man is there on the ground like a sleeping child.

THE LIGHTHOUSE KEEPER LOVES BIRDS TOO MUCH

Birds in their thousands fly toward the lights
in their thousands they fall in their thousands they crash
in their thousands blinded in their thousands stunned
in their thousands they die

The lighthouse keeper can't stand that kind of thing
he loves birds too much
so he says Dammit, that does it!

And he turns off everything

In the distance a cargo ship is wrecked
a cargo ship coming from the tropics
a cargo ship loaded with birds
thousands of birds from the tropics
thousands of drowned birds.

DOCKER'S HEART

Docker's heart
That's the name of my song

It takes place in Antwerp or Hamburg or Dunkirk

The docker is standing on the wharf
on his chest instead of his heart
another heart is tattooed
It's the heart of the heartless girl
and below her story is set out

Her father had heart trouble
her mother was heartily troubled

One fine day, St. Whosit's Day
the heartless girl is in hospital
and the docker has stopped at the door
and has some oranges in his hands

But the girl has died
and the docker opens his hands

Roll oranges, roll in the gutter
In the harbour you will rot with the old pieces of cork

Portrait of the heartless girl
On a heart-shaped medallion
at the back of a drawer you lie there
and the docker has an aching heart
in a corridor he fell down
and all the girls around him begin to cry

Outside
there's the travelling fair
the candy the music
and the merry-go-round
And everything began to go round
memories came back

Memories
you scratch the heart of the poor docker
and you take him by the hand
and you lead him to where his girl used to work

And by the bed the man fell down

Outside
is the wailing of the merry-go-round

Horses with blue and badly painted eyes
horses with a horsehair mane
you go around in circles without ever getting drunk
and you never say anything
But heart-rending and heart-broken
the music goes on non-stop

Wooden songs for the wooden horses
Iron songs for the iron horse
the music is still music
sometimes good sometimes bad

The heart takes heart
in search of another heart
how it is sentimental in the Spring
how it beats when it hears a love song

Heart of a docker
That's the name of my song.

WHEN YOU SLEEP

You sleep at night
but I have insomnia
I see you sleeping
that hurts me

Your eyes closed your big body stretched out
it's funny but that makes me cry
and suddenly you are laughing
you roar with laughter while you're sleeping
wherever are you at this moment
wherever have you gone really
perhaps with another woman
far away in another country
and being with her you're laughing at me

You sleep at night
but I have insomnia
I see you sleeping
that hurts me

When you're asleep I don't know if you love me
You're very near but still so far
I'm naked pressed close against you
but it's like I wasn't there
yet I hear your beating heart
I don't know if it's beating for me
I don't know anything I know nothing more
I'd like your heart to stop beating
if there ever came a day when you stopped loving me

You dream at night
but I have insomnia
I see you dreaming
that makes me cry

Every night I cry all night
and you, you dream and you smile
but that can't go on
surely one night I'll kill you
your dreams will be finished then
and as I'll kill myself too
my insomnia will also be over
our two corpses side by side
will sleep together in our double bed

You dream at night
but I have insomnia
I see you dreaming
that makes me cry

Here's daylight and suddenly you wake up
and it's me you smile at
you smile with the sunshine
and I stop thinking about the night
you always say the same words
"Did you have a good night"
and I reply like the day before
"Yes my darling I slept well
and I dreamed of you like every night."

ANYTHING TO PASS THE TIME

To Agnès Capri

People think it's easy
to do nothing at all
in fact it's hard
it's as hard as anything
you have to pass the time
it's a real job
you have to pass the time
it's a labour of Hercules

Ah!
from morning till night
I did nothing
nothing
ah! what a funny thing
from morning till night
from night until morning
I did the same thing
nothing!
I did nothing
I could afford to
ah! what a sad story
I could have had it all
yes
what I had wanted
if I had wanted it
I could have had
but there was nothing I fancied
nothing

However one day I saw a dog
this dog that I liked I got
it was a big dog
a sheepdog
but the poor animal
how he was bored

he missed his master
an old Scotsman
I bought his master
I could afford it
ah!
what an odd echo
oh!
what an odd Scotsman he was
my dog's shepherd
all day long he wept
all night he sobbed
ah!
he was utterly mad

The Scotsman wasted away
he wouldn't listen to anything
he even talked about hanging himself
I prefer my sheep
he sang in Scots
and the dog barked
hearing him sing
I could afford it
I bought the sheep
I put them in my living room
So they ate my rugs
and then they died of boredom
and the Scotsman followed them
into the grave
ah!
and the dog too

That's when I left on a cruise

To-calm-my-little-nerves.

KISS ME

It was in a district of the City of Light
Where it's always dark where there's never any air
In winter and summer it's always winter there
She was on the stair
He was beside her she was beside him
It was night
It smelled of sulphur
Because they'd been killing bedbugs that afternoon
And she said to him
It's dark here
There's no air
Winter and summer it's always winter
God's sun doesn't shine our way
It has far too much to do in the rich neighbourhoods
Hold me in your arms
Kiss me
Kiss me for a long time
Kiss me
Later it will be too late
Our life is now
Here everything kills you
The heat and the cold
You freeze you suffocate
You can't get any air
If you stopped kissing me
I think I would suffocate
You're fifteen and I'm fifteen
So we're thirty together
At thirty you're not children any more
You're old enough to work
And old enough to kiss each other
Later it will be too late
Our life is now
Kiss me!

SONG OF THE GLAZIER

How fine it is
what you can see just like that
through the sand through the glass
through the window panes
here look for example
how fine it is
that woodcutter
way over there
who is cutting down a tree
to make planks
for the joiner
who has to make a big bed
for the little flower-seller
who is going to marry
the lamplighter
who lights the street lamps every evening
so that the cobbler can see
to repair the shoes of the shoe-shine boy
who brushes those of the knife-grinder
who sharpens the scissors of the hairdresser
who cuts the hair of the bird seller
who gives his birds to everyone
to put everyone in a good mood.

THE YOUNG LION IN A CAGE

A young lion grew up in captivity, and as he got bigger, so did the bars of his cage, at least that's what the young lion thought... in reality they changed his cage while he was asleep.

Sometimes men came and threw dust in his eyes, at other times they hit him on the head with a stick and he thought, "They're vicious and stupid, but they could be more so; they killed my father, they killed my mother, they killed my brothers, one day they will surely kill me. What are they waiting for?"

And he waited too.

And nothing happened.

Another day dawned. The workmen of the zoo place benches in front of the cage. Some visitors come in and sit down.

The lion looks at them curiously.

The visitors are seated... they seem to be waiting for something... a ticket inspector comes to see if they all have tickets... there is an argument, a little man has sat down in the front row... he doesn't have a ticket... so the ticket inspector throws him out, kicking him in the belly... all the others applaud.

The lion finds it very entertaining and thinks that humans have become kinder and that they have simply come just to have a casual look in passing.

"That's a good ten minutes that they've been here," he thinks, "and nobody has hurt me. That is remarkable. They're merely paying me a simple visit. I would really like to do something for them...

But the door of the cage is abruptly thrown open and a man appears yelling, "Hey Sultan! Up Sultan!"

And the lion is filled with a justified uneasiness, for he has never seen a lion-tamer before.

The lion-tamer has a chair in his hand. He hits the chair on the bars of the cage, on the lion's head, and here and there in general. One leg of the chair breaks, the man throws the chair down, and taking a big revolver out of his pocket, he begins to fire it in the air.

"What?" says the lion. "what's all this? The one time I have company, this madman turns up, a fanatic who comes in here without knocking, who breaks up the furniture and shoots at my guests! That's not the way to behave." And jumping on the lion-tamer, he starts to devour him, more out of a desire to introduce a bit of order than pure gluttony...

Some of the spectators faint; most run for it. The rest rush to the cage and drag the lion-tamer by the feet, nobody knows quite why; but that's panic for you.

The lion doesn't understand what's going on. His guests hit him with their umbrellas. There's a dreadful hubbub.

An Englishman is still sitting by himself in his corner and is saying over and over, "I saw it coming. It had to happen. Ten years ago I predicted it..."

Whereupon all the others turn on him and shout, "What did you say? Everything that's happened is all your fault, you filthy foreigner, have you even paid for your seat?" And so on.

And at that the Englishman also gets hit with some umbrellas.

"He's having a bad day, too," thinks the lion.

THE FIRST ASSES

In former times asses were completely wild, that is, they ate when they were hungry, they drank when they were thirsty, and they ran around in the grass when they felt like it.

Sometimes a lion would come and eat an ass; then all the other asses would run away crying like asses, but the next day they forgot all about it and went back to braying, drinking, eating, running, sleeping... In short, except for the days when the lion came, everything went along fairly well.

One day the lords of creation (that's what humans like to call themselves when they're talking together) arrive in the land of the asses and the asses, very pleased to have some new company, gallop to meet the humans.

THE ASSES
(They speak as they gallop.)

They are strange, pale animals, they walk on two hooves, their ears are very small, they are not handsome, but all the same we ought to give them a little welcome. It's the least we can do.

And the asses clown round, they roll in the grass waving their hooves, they sing the song of the asses and then just for a joke, they push the humans to make them ever so slightly fall over. But humans don't very much like joking when they aren't the ones making the joke, and the lords of creation weren't in the land of the asses five minutes before all the asses were tied up like sausages.

All, that is, except for the youngest, the tenderest. That one is killed and roasted on a spit, and the men stand around him with knives in their hands. When the ass is done to a turn, the men begin to eat and make bad-tempered grimaces, then throw down their knives.

ONE OF THE HUMANS
(He speaks alone)

It's not as good as beef, it's not as good as beef!

ANOTHER

It's no good, I like mutton better!

ANOTHER

Ugh, this is terrible!
(He cries)

And the captive asses, seeing the man cry, think that it's remorse that causes his tears.

"They're going to let us go," think the asses; but the men get up and all talk among themselves gesticulating emphatically.

CHORUS OF HUMANS

These animals are not good to eat, their voices are unpleasant, their ears ridiculously long, they are certainly stupid and don't know either how to read or how to count. We will call them asses because that's what we feel like calling them, and they will carry our baggage. We are the lords of creation. Onward!

And the men lead the asses away.

OF OUR FIRST PARENTS...

Cain and Abel had one sister, whom they called Whore and
Rebel.
One fine day they killed each other over her.
"This is getting off to a good start," says Adam.
"Think so?" says Eve smiling.
"Still all the same, you must admit that it's tragic!" says Adam.
"Tragedy isn't such a big deal," says Eve.
"Just an absence of good breeding."

And she went back to musing.
Now and then the serpent, like a good, well mannered little dog,
                brought her the apple that Eve sometimes deigned
                              to throw for him.

RUBY HEART

I know how to say "I love you"
but I don't know how to love
Your ruby heart
what have I done with it?

I played at love
I didn't even know how to play
Your ruby heart
what have I done with it?

The window is broken
the shop closed
the satin torn
the jewel case trampled on

I wanted to have you
I wanted to possess you
I was playing at love
I only cheated

Your ruby heart
what have I done with it?
Now it's too late
I've wrecked everything

Your ruby heart
I can't even flog it off
There's no fence
for stolen love.

HONEYMOON

Oh it's her... it's her says the man
I recognise her
the woman I've been searching for for years
the one who's always in my dreams
that's her I recognise her
she's sitting on a bench
and she's crying
The man goes up to her and asks questions
I love a man and he loves me
so I'm crying
says the woman
Oh that's not true love says the man
give me this man's address
I'm going to take care of it
And he goes there
five minutes
the time it takes to see the man and kill him
to close the door and go away
When he returns the woman is already in mourning
and ready for the trip
she smiles
they go away
but death is hidden in their luggage
They arrive
they sleep
they wake up
the man looks at the woman
and he is absolutely knocked sideways
Oh it's not her
she has grey eyes
she has a slight nasal twang
oh it's not her
she's not the one I was looking for
I've made a mistake.

LOST PROPERTY OFFICE

Complaint

"Oh Officer...
Oh Officer...!!!"

"Yes, well, what is it?"

"Oh Officer
I've lost...I've lost"

"Well...what...speak up...say something
my time is valuable
what have you lost?"

"Officer
I have lost my brother in the war"

"That is unfortunate but what does that have to do with me?"

"It has a lot to do with me
Officer
and that is why I am here
it's a crime
there was a crime

a crime... listen to me

I'm lodging a complaint

listen to me

an enquiry must be made
an enquiry must be made
it's your job to search
you have to search

go on get on your feet go out
put on your sash of office
take fingerprints... take your dog...

do something
get up... get a move on... shake a leg

go out
run
search
it's your job to search
you have to search
my brother has been killed
it's a crime
I'm lodging a complaint
you have to listen to me

what's that you say?

the case is closed!
It's more like a cover-up
sir"

"You are talking my arm off."

"You don't need that arm
officer
but my brother is missing an arm
or maybe both of them
he has disappeared
nobody knows where...
all anyone knows is that he's dead
if he weren't dead
he would have come back
What you're smiling
ironically
sir
and your dog

is smiling too
–slavishly–
what did you say?
that I'm lodging a complaint against a person unknown
but you're crazy
and your dog's crazy too
come on
I tell you I know the guilty men
I tell you I know the names

listen to me
I'm going to say the names
first of all
the committee of the iron-works... Mr. de Wendel
the...
oh let me speak
oh... but...
oh... let me... let me... ah..."

"Special hospital," says the officer.

DISAPPOINTMENT

or

GOING FISHING

A dead man on the river bank
a very calm dead man who is fishing
Suddenly he turns pale:
I say where have I put my maggots
...I must have left them at home
and he goes back to the graveyard
but the gate is locked
I say where have I put my key
I must have left it on the river bank
He goes back
and sees the key at the bottom of the river
Oh he says it has fallen in
they ought to make keys out of cork
that way they could float
if I leave it at the bottom of the river
it is surely going to get rusty
He dives in
A big live fish
rushes at him and eats him
Life is really just
one damned thing after another
says the dead man...

Not much flesh
lots of bones
thinks the fish

YOU LEFT ME

You left me my dear
As I left you
We left each other together
Each one individually
It was to hear each other better
and miss each other very much
It was to understand each other
to know who we were

You are as lovely as the day
the day when for the first time I caught
sight of you and as sad as the night
when you left without a second thought

TRANSLATOR'S NOTES

p. 13. 'The Horse's Story' was composed in 1933 to be recited by the Groupe Octobre.

p. 16. 'Whale Fishing' was written in 1933 for Groupe Octobre while Prévert was on a trip to Czechoslovakia; he wrote 'Kiss Me' at the same time. Set to music by Joseph Kosma and sung by Agnès Capri in 1936, it was a great hit, but it wasn't published until 1941.

p. 28. 'Hamlet at School' contains two translation difficulties. One is the fact that Hamlet begins conjugating the verb 'to be' in English and the teacher berates him for not conjugating 'être', that is, the verb 'to be' in French. It does not make sense in the translation to reverse these languages and have Hamlet begin to conjugate the verb in French, so I have substituted the language Hamlet might logically be expected to conjugate verbs in: Danish.

The title of the poem in French is 'L'accent grave'. The joke is not only on a 'grave accent', a solemn speaking tone, but the grave accent in French, which is a diacritical mark over certain vowels which can change the meaning of a homonym. As 'ou' means 'or' and 'où' means 'where', Hamlet may be saying either 'I am or I am not' or 'I am where I am not'.

p. 29. "Pater Noster". The Ourcq Canal is 108 km long and flows partly through Paris; it connects the Ourcq River with the Seine. The Morlaix River is a small river in Brittany.

p. 31. 'The Return Home'. First published in 1937, 'The Return Home' is based on a real story of a 19th-century murderer, a man named Lacenaire. As he and his father were walking past the scene of a public execution, his father predicted that young Lacenaire would end up on the scaffold. The prediction haunted the boy, who had never previously misbehaved or been in trouble. He is supposed to have said that from that moment there was an invisible link connecting him with the guillotine. Prévert uses this story again in his film, 'Les Enfants du Paradis'. Vaugirard is a district in south Paris; the rue Vaugirard is the longest street in the city.

p. 33. 'The Concert Was not a Success'. Written in 1943. Prévert is dealing with the problem of the artist writing about ugly, uncomfortable things. The 'companions of the bad days' refers to the friends he was living with during the Occupation.

p. 35. 'Days of Dregs and Thorns'. The French title of this is 'Time of Cherry Stones' and is a parody of a 19th-century song about the Paris Commune called 'Time of Cherries' (*Temps de cerises*). The military barracks in the rue de la Pepinière still exists. Monsieur Babylas is a character in a one-act comic opera called 'Monsieur Choufleury Will Stay at Home on January 24' by Saint-Rémy and Offenbach. Babylas was the neighbour of the heroine, Ernestine, who sings 'Cher Babylas!/Hélas! Hélas!' as she considers him as a lover. 'Son of St. Louis rise to heaven' are reputedly the words of Louis XVI's chaplain as the king was about to be executed.

p. 41. 'Into my House'. Written during the War in the house Prévert rented in Tourette-sur-Loup in the south of France.

p. 44. 'Song in the Blood' couldn't be published during the Occupation, but it appeared in April 1945 and was promptly set to music by Joseph Kosma. Prévert had written it in 1936.

p. 46. 'Wash Day'. The French proverb, 'You must wash your dirty linen at home', is similar to the English one: 'Don't wash your dirty linen in public'. Prévert often takes the literal meaning of a cliché or common saying and plays with it, like an extended pun. The attack on hypocrisy is typical of Prévert; the family would commit murder to preserve the appearance of respectability.

p. 52. 'The Musicians'. The French title of this poem, 'L'Orgue de Barbarie', is the key to an elaborate pun. A 'Barbary Organ' is a hurdy-gurdy, but it can also mean a 'barbaric organ'.

p. 56. 'Breakfast'. One of Prévert's simplest poems and also one of the most discussed and analysed. First published in March 1945, the poem is startlingly cinematographic, as many of Prévert's poems are. The speaker is usually taken to be the wife or mistress of the silent man, but we don't know for sure. It could be a male lover or a mother, for instance.

p. 60. 'To Make a Portrait of a Bird'. Elsa Henriquez, to whom Prévert dedicated this poem, was a young artist mounting her first exhibition in Monaco in 1943 when he wrote this. Later, after the War, she often illustrated Prévert's texts.

p. 64. 'Sacred Scriptures'. This poem was published in 1943 in a review called *Méridien* and caused such a scandal that bookshops refused to stock the magazine and subscribers cancelled their subscriptions.

p. 68. 'The Broken Mirror'. Prévert's mother died in February 1945, and the poem is thought to refer to her and to Prévert's childhood in Neuilly-sur-Seine.

p. 68. 'Taking Liberties'. Although this popular poem was published first in September 1943 in a student magazine and then in December 1945 in *La Revue internationale*, it had circulated privately before that.

p. 71. 'The Message'. Like the very visual, cinema-like 'Breakfast', 'The Message' is deeply ambiguous. It it impossible to be sure whether one or two people are involved.

p. 73. 'Vincent's Lament' was published in December 1944. Vincent Van Gogh cut part of his left ear off and gave it to a prostitute. The following day (Christmas Eve, 1888) the police found him unconscious in his bed and took him to a hospital. He was discharged on 7 January 1889 and went back to work painting.

Paul Eluard was the pen name of Eugène Émile Grindel (1895-1952), a poet known for his work in the wartime Resistance and later membership in the Communist Party. He was an early surrealist and a highly-regarded love poet.

p. 74. *'Paris at Night'*. The title is in English in the original.

p. 75. 'Barbara'. One of Prévert's most famous songs. The Germans occupied Brest from 18 June 1940 and made it an important naval base. It suffered 65 bombardments during the next four years and was further flattened during its liberation. The poem was banned from the radio in 1945 because it was a sensitive subject as the War was still being fought. (It was finally published in 1947.) The censors particularly objected to his line 'What sheer bloody stupidity war is!' *(Quelle connerie la guerre)*. Prévert chose the name Barbara because he had heard it in Brittany and thought it was rather exotic, since it is not a common French name.

p. 77. 'Inventory'. Prévert wrote a similar poem in 1938 called 'Statistics' and another version was set to music by Joseph Kosma and published in 1946. Still another version had appeared in 1944 in a magazine. Prévert wrote and rewrote his 'Inventory', giving a lot of time and thought to these seemingly disparate items; they are not quite as random as they seem at first. This poem is so well known in France that it has entered the language in the phrase 'an inventory à la Prévert'.

p. 83. 'Procession'. As in 'Inventory', the combinations are not entirely random and accidental. *Toilers of the Sea* is a novel by Victor Hugo. The death's head hussars were German guard regiments created in the 18th century and disbanded in 1918. Their fur headgear was decorated with a skull.

p. 91. 'Public Confession'. The punning subtitle in French is *'Loto Critique'* which sounds like *l'auto-critique*, or self-criticism, and reflects the mood of guilt and self-criticism of the French in 1940 and afterwards. *The Terrible Year* is a collection of poems by Victor Hugo; the reference is to 1871 and the defeat of the French in the Franco-Prussian War. The poem is dated from Jurançon, near Pau, where Prévert fled from occupied Paris in August 1940.

p. 93. 'The Betrayed Lovers'. The pun in the French text involves the double meaning of 'to sell the wick', which also means to let the cat out of the bag. A literal translation would be: 'I had a lamp / and you the light / Who sold the wick?'

p. 98. 'Song for You' is dedicated to Florence Loeb, the daughter of an art dealer, whom Prévert knew in Antibes.

p. 105. 'Song of the Shoeshine Boys' was inspired by Prévert's sojourn in New York in 1938, where he often visited Harlem to hear the jazz in the nightclubs there.

p. 110. 'Docker's Heart' went through many different versions from its first appearance as a song in 1936 until its eventual publication in 1953. As Prévert reworked the poem, it became more concise until finally it is not clear that the woman is a prostitute whom the docker has made pregnant and who is dying in a hospital from a miscarriage or abortion.

p. 114. 'Anything to Pass the Time'. Agnès Capri was a cabaret singer who sang many of Prévert's songs.

p. 117. 'Song of the Glazier' was sung for the first time by Charles Trénet in *Adieu Léonard*, a film devised by Prévert's brother Pierre.